My Life

My Life

The life and times of Lloyd Ray Bowyer

L. RAY BOWYER

authorHOUSE®

AuthorHouse™
1663 Liberty Drive
Bloomington, IN 47403
www.authorhouse.com
Phone: 1-800-839-8640

First published by AuthorHouse   10/21/2011

ISBN: 978-1-4670-9470-2 (sc)
ISBN: 978-1-4670-9468-9 (ebk)

Library of Congress Control Number: 2011919227

Printed in the United States of America

Any people depicted in stock imagery provided by Thinkstock are models, and such images are being used for illustrative purposes only.
Certain stock imagery © Thinkstock.

This book is printed on acid-free paper.

PREFACE

I have led a very common life, but I feel the record of that life might be of some interest to a few people, so I am motivated to record my memories. I start with a brief summary of the lives of my parents, to provide some background information.

For younger readers, I would like to mention some of the differences between my childhood and today. Computers and television did not exist. Hand calculators did not exist, so all computation was by pencil and paper. We had cars, but the cars didn't have air conditioning or automatic transmissions—the transmission had to be shifted manually. Every car had a crank to use to start the engine, in case the electric starter failed. Airplanes existed, but they all had propellers—no jet engines. Telephones existed, but they had no dials or buttons. When you picked up the handset, an operator said, "Number please," and after you told the operator the number, she would set up the connection. (Operators were always women.) We had radio, but it was only AM—FM had been invented, but it wasn't in public use. Microwaves didn't exist, so of course microwave ovens didn't exist. Photography existed, both still and movie, but it was black and white, on film. Color processing didn't exist, and digital images didn't exist. Air conditioning existed for some public buildings, but no one had air conditioning at home.

Ray Bowyer
10549 Big Canoe
Big Canoe, Georgia 30143
October 14, 2011

Ralph Willis Bowyer

My father, Ralph Willis Bowyer, was born in Wright, Kansas, on December 7, 1907, the eighth of eleven children. The family moved to Kiowa County, Colorado, near Eads, in 1916. The life of the family in both Kansas and Colorado is recorded in a booklet[1]. The family had very limited resources, and Ralph learned to make do with little, and to be self-reliant. His mother died in 1921, and the housekeeping became the responsibility of Ralph's older sisters.

In the fall of 1923, Ralph moved to Eads to enter high school. From that point on, he was totally on his own. He graduated from Eads High School in 1927, and enrolled in the Colorado State College of Education (now the University of Northern Colorado). When he graduated, in 1933, the depression was on, and schools were not hiring many teachers. He worked at different times for a Firestone Tire Store and the College, in the Buildings and Grounds Department. In my earliest memory, he was working at Hanson's Greenhouse, where the family had an apartment over the customer area of the greenhouse.

Ralph met Susie Skavdahl, my mother, while he was in college. They were married August 19, 1934, at her parent's home in Sioux County, Nebraska.

Ralph had joined the Colorado National Guard while he was in college, and his unit was activated in September, 1940. His division went on to fight in Europe, but he was separated from the division and made

---

[1] <u>Reminiscences of Pioneer Life</u>, by John Riley Bowyer, Ralph Willis Bowyer, Florence Doonan, Betty Lee Jacobs, and Viola Rose—May 6, 2003

part of a "cadre," a group of officers sent to a base to organize a new division. Each new division was trained to be ready for combat, and sent off to fight, while the cadre went to a new base to start a new division.

Susie Blanche Skavdahl

My mother, Susie Blanche Skavdahl, was born in Harrison, Nebraska, on November 15, 1907, the oldest of seven children. Her father, Oscar Skavdahl, was born in Norway, and came to North America as a child. Her childhood was spent on the ranch in Sioux County, Nebraska, which her father had carved out of open prairie. The ranch is still in the family, and is currently being operated by my first cousin, Charles Skavdahl.

In 1920, Oscar and his wife, Grace, moved the family to Boulder County, Colorado, near Longmont. We think it was probably because they thought schools would be better there. In 1925, they moved back to Sioux County, partly because the purchaser of the ranch in Sioux County was not able to keep up with payments. Susie attended high school in Miltonvale, Kansas, graduating as salutatorian in 1926. She then taught for one year, before attending Colorado State College of Education (now the University of Northern Colorado) in Greeley, Colorado. She graduated June 9, 1934, and married my father August 19, 1934.

EARLY YEARS

Baby Ray

I was born April 18, 1935, in Longmont, Colorado. My parents were living in Greeley at the time. My mother told people she went to Longmont for the birth because she liked a doctor there, who had served the family when they lived near Longmont earlier.

Ralph, Susie, and Ray

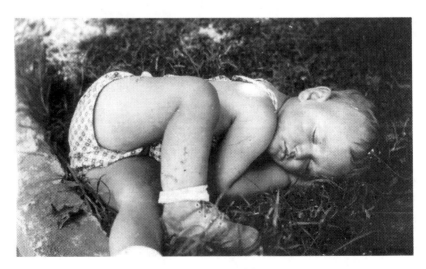

One Year Old

Three Years Old

My sister, Twyla Ruth Bowyer, was born May 31, 1938. In 1939, we moved from the greenhouse to a home at 1909 Sixth Avenue in Greeley. The house was much more spacious than the apartment over the greenhouse, and it had a nice yard for two small children to play in.

House at 1909 6th Avenue

Ray and Twyla, about five and two

WAR YEARS

In September, 1940, the Colorado National Guard was placed on active duty, and sent to Fort Sill, Oklahoma, for maneuvers. Our parents loaded Twyla and me, and most of our belongings, into our 1934 Plymouth, and we went along. Our home was in Lawton, Oklahoma. My father was transferred to Fort Benning, Georgia, and we moved to Phenix City, Alabama, in December, 1940. The pattern continued, with stays in the following places:

March, 1941, to Abilene, Texas
August, 1941, returned to Greeley
September, 1941, to Columbus, Georgia
January, 1942, to Abilene, Texas
February, 1942, to LeCompte, Louisiana
July, 1942, to Paduka, Kentucky
August, 1942, to Sturgis, Kentucky.

Early in our stay in Phenix City, Alabama, I answered the telephone, and the call was for my mother. The caller asked her, "Who was that impolite person?" A few months later, a similar call took place, and the caller asked, "Who was that polite person?" The first caller had interpreted my northern accent as impolite, and by the second I had adapted to the culture.

During our stay in Paduka, Kentucky, my father told me at one point that electricity works by coming out of one slot on the wall outlet, and going back into the other slot. That fascinated me, so I borrowed a hair-pin from my mother, and put the two legs of the hair-pin into the two slots of a wall outlet. The result was pretty spectacular.

Ray and Twyla in 1942 (in Lecompte, Louisiana)

I have always loved to read, and when I was a child, I did as much reading as I could. I think it was in Sturgis, Kentucky, that I read every single book in the children's section of the local library.

I had not seen snow from the time we left Greeley until the first winter in Sturgis, Kentucky. When the first snow fell that winter, I gazed at it out of the school window in amazement.

In 1943, the United States Military decided to set up a training operation in India to train Chinese soldiers in how to operate and maintain military equipment, for use against the Japanese. My father was chosen for this duty, and of course the family couldn't go to India, so we returned to Greeley, where we lived in the same house we had lived in three years before. I assume it had been rented out while we were away. Although my father was sorry to be so far from his family, he really enjoyed learning about another culture, and his letters were fascinating to read. To save weight and space, many letters were sent by what was called "v-mail." They were microfilmed at the originating post office, the microfilm was sent to near the destination, and then they were photographically reproduced. As a result, many of our letters were on photographic paper.

I wrote the following in a diary:

Daddy left in December 1943. He went to a base in India where they had an American school to teach the Chinese war tactics and how to use American equipment. Daddy taught the Chinese how to use our trucks.

On August 24, 1944, we went to Eads to visit the relatives. While we were there we went swimming in the lake. There was a raft out in some deep water. I walked out as far as I could and then started swimming. As the water was dirty, I kept my eyes shut. When I felt like I should be about to the raft, I stopped swimming and looked around. I had swum right past it! I nearly drowned getting turned around and swimming back.

On June 3, Daddy got a two-week leave and we went to Fontana [California] to visit some relatives. On the way back we went through Los Angeles. I got a chance to swim in the ocean in Santa Monica. I liked it very much.

Typical of parents who had lived through the depression, mine were very careful of resources. We were expected to take some of each type of food available on the table, and to eat every bite that was on our plates. The thing I liked best about the return to Colorado in 1943 was that I didn't have to eat okra any more.

While in Greeley, I joined Cub Scouts, and participated in youth baseball. I also learned to swim at the college pool. I attended the "training school," a school run by the college for the purpose of giving student teachers an opportunity to practice, and for the professors to try out their new ideas. One of the new ideas was that report cards weren't useful, and instead the teachers should write letters to the parents telling how the students were doing. The letters about me mentioned that I made some careless mistakes in arithmetic.

During this time in Greeley, I worked as a golf caddy. The Greeley Country Club was about five miles from our house. I would hitch-hike to the country club, caddy for players, and hitch-hike back home. That was certainly a more innocent time than the time we live in now.

Here are some entries in a booklet I wrote in 1944:

Over the vacation we were camping in Wibb's back yard. Wibb is a boy who lives down the street from us.

We made toy guns and played like we were Marines in the Pacific Ocean. We made a fire and put two sticks in the ground, one on each side of the fire. We put a pole across these two and hung a pan there. After awhile, when the pan got hot, I got nosey and put my finger on the pan. "Ouch!"

Some girls that live down the street have a sled. We went over to Jackson Field[2]. The side we wanted did not have enough snow on it, so we took the other side that had bumps on it.

When I came home from school I happened to come in the back door. My little sister said, "We have a surprise". It was a surprise. When I went into the living room, my daddy was there. He had come from Camp Breckner, Alabama. He had changed to his civilian clothes. I liked them better than his army clothes. He stayed a week with us. He went back on the train. I wished he could have stayed until Christmas.

I had a baby sister Friday night at 6:00. It was 7 ½ pounds when it was born. I have not seen it, but my grandmother did and she said that it does not look like my other sister or me. We have not named her yet.

---

[2] Jackson Field was the football field of the College, located across the street from our house. My friends and I often went there to play.

About January 28, my Daddy sent some French paper money. One is 20 Francs, or 40 cents, and the other is 5 Francs, or 10 cents. On the top of each it says, "Banque De L'Algerie", or translated, Bank of Algiers. We think my Daddy is in Oran, Algieria.

Over the vacation the best surprise I had was that my grandmother brought a turkey when she came. She came because my mother was sick with the flu.

My younger sister, Anita Grace Bowyer, was born January 7, 1944. Since our father was in India, they didn't see each other until she was almost two years old.

Ray, Twyla, and Anita in 1945

In November, 1945, it was no longer necessary to train Chinese soldiers, so my father was reassigned to Fort Ord, California, and we moved to the small town of Marina, California. This time, he was already in California at the time we moved, so my mother drove the distance with the three young children. It was exciting for me, although it was probably very stressful for her. She had studied weather forecasts prior to leaving, but forgot to check on the last day. We got only as far as Larkspur, about 150 miles from Greeley, when a snowstorm brought our trip to a stop. We stayed in a motel with cracks in the walls that let the snow blow in, but we had a wood-burning stove, so we were reasonably comfortable. I remember the excitement of crossing Raton Pass, and a stop at the petrified forest in Arizona.

Here's another entry in my diary:

At about 3:00 on November 27, we saw the store that had a sign that said "Marina." We soon found the house Daddy had described. It was a 4-room house with bath. Daddy was there waiting for us.

Marina was a village consisting of one general store and post office, three liquor joints, one 3-room school, and about a dozen houses.

It was about 10 miles from Monterey and about 2 miles from Fort Ord.

The school, which went only through eighth grade, had the old-fashioned approach of sending home report cards. When my report cards had D and F in mathematics, my mother had a fit. She started drilling me on math. I developed excellent mathematics skills that stayed with me the rest of my life. There was no Cub Scout program, but I participated in 4-H. My 4-H project was a vegetable garden.

Shortly after coming to Marina, a group of boys on the playground said to me, "We're going to find out who is boss. We'll fight you one at a time, until you win or we win." I don't remember the fight itself, so it must not have been as traumatic as the threat.

In May, 1946, my father was transferred to Camp Stoneman, California, on the east side of San Francisco bay, and we moved to Rodeo, just up the bay from Berkeley. This was a larger town, which had a Cub Scout program, so I resumed that activity. I had a paper route there, delivering the San Francisco Chronicle and the Gazette.

My friends and I walked to a beach on San Francisco Bay, about two miles from home, to swim. One of the times I was there, we were diving off a raft anchored perhaps 100 feet from the beach. On one of my dives, I went too deep, and rubbed against something (perhaps part of an anchor holding the raft in place), which cut a long gash in my chest. When I came up, I said to an adult on the raft, "Do you know where I can get some first aid?" He thought I said Band-Aid, and he responded, "You need more than a Band-Aid." He took me to a doctor, and called my mother to come meet us there. It took sixteen stitches to close the wound, and that ended my swimming for that year.

SETTLING IN HUGO

In December, 1946, my father was discharged from active duty. He drove to Colorado, to look for a business to buy. The business he found was the dry cleaners in Hugo, about 100 miles southeast of Denver. My mother cried when she learned it. She said, "He's never paid any attention to clothes. How can he make a living cleaning clothes?" The trip to Colorado was exciting for me. Since my father had taken the car, we traveled by Greyhound bus. I sat behind the driver, and he taught me a lot about driving and operating a bus. The bus broke down in the middle of the night in Utah, and we stayed by the side of the road until another bus could be sent to take us the rest of the way.

I was only in Hugo a little over six years, but I think of it as my home town. It was a wonderful place to live, and I treasure the memories of those years. There were usually about 20 people in each school class, so it was possible to do well in a variety of activities. I had been studying piano as much as possible since the second grade, and I became the church organist. I had started studying trombone in California, but I discovered trombone didn't usually play the melody, so I shifted to trumpet when

I moved to Hugo. I played in the school band the whole time I was in Hugo.

In high school, all able-bodied males were expected to play every sport, which I did. I lettered three years in football, two years in basketball, and one year in track. I was selected to go to Boys State the summer after my junior year, which is a program intended to make young leaders into good citizens. I was in every school play, usually playing the father because of my height.

I wrote the following essay as a school assignment in about the seventh grade or so:

My Ambitions

When I grow up I want to be an electrical engineer. Daddy says I would make a good electrical or architectural engineer because I like arithmetic and have the patience to work mathematical problems.

I like electricity and daddy has taught me a little bit about it. When we moved to Hugo there was one room that wasn't finished. Naturally, I got it. No one else would take it. It did not have a light in it, but there was a wire that went across the room to an outlet socket in the kitchen.

One night when I was supposed to be in bed I got an extension cord and took off the thing that you plug into the outlet, and scratched some of the insulation off the two wires, being careful not to touch both of them at the same time, because there was

120 volts in there ready to shock any dumb cluck that touched them. Then I put on my extension cord and taped it up. Thank goodness I wasn't shocked, but I got a light, anyway.

Later, when Daddy found out about it, he said that if I had touched both wires at the same time it would have thrown me clear across the room.

I continued in Cub Scouts and moved on to Boy Scouts, but I only got to Star before I dropped out. I had a wonderful experience in 1950. I had the opportunity to attend the National Boy Scout Jamboree in Valley Forge, Pennsylvania. We went on a special train, which started in Colorado Springs (Hugo was in the Pikes Peak Council, with headquarters in Colorado Springs), picked up some additional cars full of Boy Scouts in Denver, and headed east. We stopped at the Ford Museum in Michigan, saw a professional baseball game and took the around-Manhattan boat ride in New York, and stopped at the Naval Academy in Annapolis, Maryland. At the jamboree itself, we had the opportunity to meet and interact with other Scouts from around the country. There was a tent at the jamboree that had television sets playing, which was my first opportunity to see that modern wonder. President Truman spoke to us. We saw a fireworks display that exceeded any I had ever seen before. The Korean War began while I was on this trip, and that was a very significant thing to me.

Boy Scout

Once, in a football game with Stratton, I felt a crack when I was pushing really hard to block another player, and couldn't walk afterward. The team doctor looked at my foot and ankle, and said, "It will be all right. Walk around on it, and you can go back in in the second half." Well, I couldn't go back in in the second half, and X-rays disclosed a break in the ankle. So I didn't play any more football for a while.

One year, I registered for an accounting class. The school superintendent, who was also the high school principal and guidance counselor, said to me, "That class is aimed at people who will take care of the books for a small-town grocery store. You don't need that. Someday you will be an engineer, making a presentation to a board of directors to convince them to approve a project, so you need to take the course in public speaking." I accepted his advice.

In my senior year, the students decided to create the first Annual of Hugo High School. I was selected to be editor, and I enjoyed carrying out those duties.

Our House in Hugo

My only brother, Larry Dean Bowyer, was born April 9, 1948. My mother had some leg problems associated with the birth, so she was in bed quite a bit. Twyla and I were very helpful to her.

I have been active in churches all my life. When we lived in Greeley, we attended the First Methodist Church. When we lived in the South, we usually attended Baptist churches. In California, we attended Presbyterian churches. When we moved to Hugo, we became active in the Hugo United Methodist Church. I especially enjoyed the discussions of religious subjects we had at Methodist Youth Fellowship, and the meetings we would go to with MYF all around the state.

I worked at many jobs during these years. As I mentioned previously, I had some jobs in Greeley and in Marina. In Hugo, I delivered the newspaper called Grit for several years. I delivered the Rocky Mountain News for a while. I worked for the county agent in weeding an experimental plot one summer, and in mixing grasshopper poison another summer. I cleaned the floor of the cleaners for my father for several years, and I cleaned the Hugo post office for a while.

My grandfather, Oscar Skavdahl, had retired from the ranch in Nebraska, turning it over to his son, my Uncle Harold Skavdahl. Apparently, he didn't enjoy retirement, so he bought another cattle ranch near Sedalia, Colorado. In the summer of 1948, I began several years of working at cattle ranches by working for my grandfather. I was fortunate to work at a time of significant change in technology. Just before I started, all haying work was by muscle power, human or animal. The grass was mowed with a horse-drawn mower, raked with a horse-drawn rake, picked up by a horse-drawn sweep, and taken to a horse-operated stacker. At the time I started, the mower had become tractor-operated, and the sweep had been mechanized by converting pick-up trucks into sweeps. During my time, the stacker team of horses was replaced by a truck or jeep, and rakes were mechanized by connecting to tractors. Later, everything was mechanized, and the horses were relegated to use in herding cattle. In the following three years, I worked either for my grandfather or for my Uncle Harold, in Nebraska, or both. During one of the summers in Nebraska, I had an opportunity to participate in a round-up, and to help herd the cattle from the pasture to the sale barn in Harrison. That was a really exciting activity.

In the summer of 1951, I obtained a job working for a local wheat-farmer, driving a tractor all summer pulling what is called a one-way plow.

In the summers of 1952 and 1953, I worked as a life guard at the municipal swimming pool in Hugo.

I was always interested in girls, as most guys are, but during my years in Hugo, I was terrified of the possibility that I might ask for a date, get turned down, and then all my friends would say, "Ho, ho, ho, Bowyer asked for a date and got turned down." So my solution was not to ask for a date. Two events, the junior and senior proms, required a date. I solved the first one by taking a girl from Limon, a town about 15 miles away, whom I had met at an MYF district event. I solved the second one by taking a girl from Englewood, a suburb of Denver, whom I had met at an MYF state event. My life would have been richer if I had dated more, but my life was pretty full as it was.

High School Senior

I graduated from Hugo High School in 1953, second in my class of 21. I enrolled at the University of Colorado. Together with some friends,

I had become an amateur radio operator, and I had constructed several electronic kits. All this activity strengthened my interest in electronics, so I chose electrical engineering as my major.

I still love to get back to Hugo when my classmates are there, to keep up with what has happened to people. Because of limited employment opportunities in Hugo, only two of my classmates still live there. One had married the Chevrolet-Pontiac dealer in town, and the other became a rancher in the area.

My father had a strong influence on my life. Two things he stressed were total integrity, and "Always do the best you can at everything you undertake." I have followed those two ideals all my life. My mother also had a strong influence, but it was a little more subtle.

Ray, Twyla, Anita, and Dean in 1983

MARGARET JANE CLARKE

I'll now discuss the background for an important part of my life. Thomas Henry Clarke was born September 12, 1905, in Cornwall, in the southwest corner of England. He was the youngest of six children. His life story is recorded in a book he wrote[3]. He emigrated to North America in the summer of 1923, first settling in British Columbia, Canada. He then spent some time in Washington State, before arriving in Detroit,

---

[3] Memoirs of Thomas H. Clarke, by Thomas H. Clarke, published October 28, 2002.

Michigan. He had a variety of jobs, and in 1930 he was operating a Standard Oil Company service station with a partner. He was married September 12, 1931, to Isabel Lorna Clarke.

Isabel was born December 15, 1903, in Nova Scotia, Canada, the sixth of ten children. She was visiting a brother in Windsor, Ontario (across the river from Detroit) when she met Tom Clarke. They were married after a short courtship.

Tom and Isabel had two daughters. Janet Anne Clarke was born November 15, 1932, at Highland Park, Michigan. Margaret Jane Clarke was born July 2, 1935, at the same place. In 1943, Tom gave up the service station, and took a job with Welch Industries, which at that time was producing war material. In 1946, Welch Industries moved to Colorado Springs, Colorado, and Tom went there with his family to continue his employment. Later, Tom left Welch, and worked for many years for Lorig's Western Wear Store.

The family lived in a part of Colorado Springs that is a separate school district, called the Cheyenne Mountain District. Both girls graduated from Cheyenne Mountain High School and from Colorado University. Margaret, now known as Margie, graduated first in her high school class. When she enrolled at Colorado University, her major was pre-medicine.

COLLEGE YEARS

My college years were exciting, as they are for almost every college student. I lived in the dormitories all four years. I had what was called a Joint Honor scholarship, awarded to all the top graduates from Colorado high schools, which paid full tuition and fees at Colorado colleges. I worked all four years for the University Residence Halls, which paid room and board. My summer jobs provided funds for books and incidentals. My parents probably would have supported my college education, but I didn't need help, so I didn't ask for it, and they never offered.

In those days, there were men's dorms and women's dorms, and almost never did the twain meet. A couple times a year, a women's dorm would hold an open house, for the purpose of meeting boys. Boys would attend the open house, for the purpose of meeting girls. I went to such an open house, and my hostess for the open house was Margie. As we were chatting, she said, "Were you at an MYF event in Colorado Springs last year? Were you wearing a letter sweater? Were you on crutches? (I had injured a leg playing football in my senior year.) Did you have some little wire puzzles? (I had brought some little wire puzzles, mainly to see if they would attract girls, and it had worked.)" The answer to all the questions was "Yes," so we had met before—or at least, we had been in the same room before. Soon we were dating.

During my freshman year, I stayed in close contact with Denny Johnson, one of my best friends from high school, who was one year behind me. At one point, I broke an ankle playing intra-mural basketball. I sent Denny a postcard that said what I had been doing lately, and at the end, I said, "P.S. I broke my ankle yesterday." Since it was a post card, his mother read it, and called my mother to ask, "Is this some kind of a code, or did Ray really break his ankle?" I think my letter home to give the same information came a day or two later.

After I left for college, my father sold the cleaners in Hugo, and bought Longmont Motor Company in Longmont, Colorado. I assume he did it in the expectation of a larger income, but I don't think his expectation was met. He eventually closed Longmont Motor Company, and accepted a position working in Denver for the state of Colorado. Longmont was close enough to Boulder, where I was attending Colorado University, that I could go home to borrow the family car occasionally. The summers of 1954 and 1955, I lived at home in Longmont, and worked as a lifeguard at the municipal swimming facility. It was a lake, rather than a pool. Instead of being the only life guard, I was part of a team of four guards. The second summer, I was designated head life guard.

Lifeguard

The summer of 1954, Margie worked as a sales clerk at the PX at Fort Carson, near Colorado Springs, so we saw each other several times. The summer of 1955, she was selected as a participant in a Christian Leadership Seminar held in Martha's Vineyard, Massachusetts, so we didn't see each other, but there were lots of letters back and forth. By the spring of 1956, we were engaged to be married. Since, at that time, it didn't seem practical to be married and be in medical school, she changed her major from pre-medicine to combined science and education.

The summer of 1956, I accepted a position with General Electric Company in Pittsfield, Massachusetts. I worked in the Naval Ordnance Department, on an anti-aircraft missile system designed to be installed on ships. The field of work was called servo-mechanisms, and by the end of the summer, that was the specialty I wanted to pursue.

There was a tradition at that time in Colorado that friends of a wedding couple would decorate a car with "Just married" and other statements, tie tin cans to the back bumper, and other such happy things. Margie and I had set our wedding date for September 2, and I was determined to defeat the car decoration game. Margie would need a car to get to student teaching in the fall, so I bought a 1950 Oldsmobile in Pittsfield. We didn't tell anyone, and when I drove home, we told people I had found someone who wanted me to drive his car from Massachusetts to Colorado. I parked the car in the parking lot at the Broadmoor Hotel. Tom Clarke was generous enough to loan us the only family car for the honeymoon. He wondered why I wasn't very enthusiastic about washing it for the trip. After the wedding, we got a ride to our car, which was still parked at the Broadmoor, and drove away undecorated. Tom didn't have to get along without his only car, after all.

My best man was Don Gotschall, a high school friend. The ushers were Frank Peep, Ron Williams, and Bill Zimmerman, college friends, and Ken Rickard, a family friend of the Clarkes. The maid of honor was Janet Clarke, and the bridesmaids were Mary Ann Nelson, a high school friend, Janet Robertson, a college friend, and Shirley Hansord, a first cousin.

Our Wedding Picture

For our senior year, we had the job of building manager for a building, Crosman Hall, which was a married students' dormitory. I had to do some cleaning, and check apartments between tenants if anyone moved out. It was a very nice job, considering the pay was room and board for two people. Margie had a scholarship that paid tuition, fees, and books, so we still didn't need any financial help. Margie's parents sent us some money, which was greatly appreciated.

I graduated second in my class of 89 electrical engineers. I was fortunate enough to be designated Outstanding Senior Engineer, which might be considered the greatest honor I ever received. It was a good year for engineering graduates, and I had about thirty offers of employment.

My final choice was between IBM, in San Jose, California, and Bell Telephone Laboratories, in Murray Hill, New Jersey. I finally chose Bell Laboratories, partly because the offer included being supported at full salary while obtaining a Masters Degree from New York University.

EMPLOYMENT

I will cover my employment first, and then back up to cover what happened in my personal life at the same time.

The digital computer was invented in 1946 at the University of Pennsylvania, originally to do calculations of artillery trajectories for the Army. By the 1950s, versions of computers were in commercial service, mostly doing scientific calculations, and they were beginning to be used for some business calculations, primarily for accounting. In my senior year at Colorado, I started doing some reading about them, and they attracted my interest. By the end of the school year, I had given up my interest in servo-mechanisms, and decided I wanted to be involved with computers.

At Bell Laboratories, for three years I was in a training program—the first year, three days a week, the second year two days a week, and the last year one day a week. The training program had been in existence for quite a while, and my class was the first one to obtain a Master's Degree at the end of the second year. Bell Laboratories hired only about the top 10% of the graduates at the schools at which it recruited, and the NYU professors graded us pretty rigorously. Some people who had never failed at anything in their lives failed this program. I passed, but I don't think I was very high in the class. In the third year, we had Bell Laboratories instructors, and the material was primarily how the telephone business functioned.

My first work assignment was to be part of a team developing a digital computer to be manufactured by Western Electric Company for use by the Bell Telephone Companies for revenue accounting. When the project started, it was felt that the telephone companies' requirements were unique, and no computer on the market would meet those unique requirements. As time went on, our design became more and more like general-purpose digital computers, and commercial digital computers appeared more and more capable of meeting the telephone company requirements. So, in 1958, the project was terminated.

When management looked around for an appropriate assignment for the team that was freed up, they found digital communications. At the time, the best way to get digital information from one place to another was to record the information on a magnetic tape and deliver the tape to where the information was needed. An exploratory effort had just determined that it was feasible to design "data sets" (which are now called modems), which could modify digital signals from computers or similar devices to go over telephone circuits, and recover the signals at the far end to be passed on to computers or similar devices. Marketing experts had determined that there would be a good market for such devices, so we were given the job of designing data sets for production.

Working on a Data Set

It is interesting that, as I write this, my daughter-in-law, Dolores Bowyer, is one of many people working on modifying voice signals from telephones to go over digital circuits, to be recovered as voice signals on the far end. So the technology has gone full circle.

One project I worked on was particularly interesting. Most of the digital signals going from place to place at that time were not computer communication, but teletypewriter signals. People at keyboards could type, resulting in signals going through a communication medium to a distant point, where they would result in text being typed on a piece of paper. As an alternative, people or machines could take steps resulting in the punching of a paper tape. The tape could be placed in a tape reader, connected to a communication line, and at the distant end used to punch another tape or drive a printer. These signals were normally 150 bits per second or less. Since a signal at that speed was an inefficient use of a voice channel, we designed a system that could take up to six such signals, send them over one voice channel, and reconstitute the signals at the far end. It was designed and put into production, but I don't think it was used very long before such low-speed channels weren't used much, and all signals were designed for a full voice channel, or a wider-bandwidth channel than voice. It's interesting that the sets we worked on were designed for 150, 1200, 2400, or (a real stretch) 4800 bits per second. Now, standard modems routinely operate at 56,000 bits per second. This is the physical limit of a normal telephone circuit, so it will never increase. Of course, there are now ways of sending digital signals that don't use a voice telephone circuit, so the speed is not limited by the characteristics of a voice telephone circuit.

A project I was assigned at this time is a source of real pride for me. Part of our plan for data communications was that an answering data set would place a tone on the telephone circuit, at a frequency we called F2. The data set which had placed the call would detect the F2 tone, and respond with a tone at a frequency we called F1. I did the study which determined the values of F1 and F2. I believe they were 1150 hertz and 2300 hertz, respectively. I believe those two frequencies are still used today. Unfortunately, at the time I didn't recognize the value of publication, and my management didn't recommend publication, so the study is recorded only in Bell Laboratories archives, and not in any publicly available document.

In 1966, a friend of mine, Bill Highleyman, with whom I had worked for several years at Bell Laboratories, was working for a small company called Data Trends, Inc. This company did projects consisting of using general purpose digital computers, designing and manufacturing necessary supplemental hardware, writing appropriate programs, and delivering the result to a customer to meet a business need. Bill called me and suggested

I go to work for Data Trends, and I did. I did some really exciting work there, and I'll describe just one project. The Chicago Board of Trade (the place that trades in grains, beef, pork bellies, etc.) conducts its business in large open areas, called pits. At that time, an observer at each pit would write down the trades on scraps of paper, which would be used by other people to update prices on chalkboards or send them on a teletypewriter circuit (of the type I described before), which would be connected to printers all over the country, where traders would learn the current prices. Our system was designed to have a small terminal at the pit, where the reporter would enter the prices on a keyboard instead of writing them on scraps of paper. The information from the reporter's keyboard would come into our program, and the program would drive digital displays, replacing the chalk boards, and electronically drive the ticker line that went all across the country. We designed, built, and installed the system, and it did what it was supposed to do. There have probably been several succeeding generations of systems since then.

When I left Bell Laboratories, Jake Schaefer, one of the managers I knew well, said to me, "If things don't work out for you there, call us." After a couple years, I grew dissatisfied with how things were going at Data Trends, so I called Jake. True to his word, he made arrangements for me to interview several different organizations within Bell Laboratories. After the interviews, I accepted a position with the military part of Bell Laboratories, working on what became the Safeguard Ballistic Missile Defense System. The function of this system was to detect incoming ballistic missiles, separate the real warheads from the junk and chaff, and send up defensive missiles to destroy the warheads. The project was the most exciting technical opportunity I ever had. My role in the project was to plan the command, control, and communications. One part of this role was to plan the physical path of what was called the Permissive Action

Link. The Permissive Action Link was required because our defensive missiles were to have nuclear warheads. The Permissive Action Link was to go from the president (or his delegate), to the North American Aerospace Defense System (NORAD) in Cheyenne Mountain, Colorado, and from there to the system command posts in North Dakota. The visits to Cheyenne Mountain to plan this physical path also gave me a chance to visit Tom and Isabel Clarke, my in-laws.

I had been promoted to supervisor while I was working on data communications. When I returned to Bell Laboratories, I wasn't given supervisor responsibility right away, because the company never hired people into supervisor positions. After a few months, I was again promoted to supervisor. In 1972, I was offered a position at the next level of management, called Department Head. The position was in Business Information Systems. The Business Information Systems organization had been created in 1967, originally as part of AT&T. The plan was that subject matter experts would be brought in from the telephone companies on rotational assignments. These experts would write requirements, which contract programmers would implement, then the programs would be delivered to the telephone companies, and in about five years the telephone companies would be computerized. After five years, it was realized that the job was a little bit bigger than estimated. The decision was made to move the work to Bell Laboratories, and many of the people brought from the telephone companies on rotational assignments, and many of the contract programmers, would be replaced by Bell Laboratories employees. I was one of the Bell Laboratories managers who replaced a rotational manager. I continued in this part of the organization, and at this level, for the rest of my career. The organization went through many changes of name.

I'll describe just three of the many projects I worked on. One project, called TIRKS (for Trunks Integrated Record Keeping System), was designed to keep track of all the connections between central offices, called trunks, and all the piece parts that make up the trunks. It would be designed so, when a new trunk was needed, TIRKS would find the necessary parts in inventory, and issue the work orders to connect the parts to create the new trunk. Or, when an existing trunk was no longer needed, TIRKS would issue the work orders to disconnect the parts, and make them available for future use.

Another project, called Work Force Administration, would receive orders for installation or repair work, analyze the amount of time and job skills needed to accomplish the installation or repair, assign the work to craft people, and print out the assignments for the craft people to accomplish the task.

A project, which was a little bit out of the normal scope of the Business Information Systems area, was called the Service Control Point, or SCP. Normal telephone numbers carry within themselves the information needed to route a call—the area code identifies the part of the country, the central office code (the next three digits) identifies the particular building and switch, and the last four digits identify the particular line. An 800 number, however, doesn't carry such information. A particular number could be in New York, and the next sequential number could be in California. Some other means must be used to route the call. This is done by utilizing the SCP. The telephone equipment at or near the origination of the call sends a digital signal to the SCP, which has within it tables saying how each 800 number should be routed. The SCP looks up the solution in its tables, and sends a message back to the starting point, saying how the call should be routed. Since the functions of the SCP must be carried out on every call, while the person who placed the call waits, it had very stringent requirements for speed, accuracy, and reliability. We developed the system, and it was placed in service, meeting all its requirements.

On December 31, 1983, the Bell System consisted of AT&T, 23 operating telephone companies, Western Electric Company, and Bell Telephone Laboratories. All the organizations were ultimately responsible to the AT&T board of directors. On January 1, 1984, under a court order, the Bell System went out of existence. It was replaced by AT&T and seven Regional Bell Operating Companies, made out of combinations of the 23 operating telephone companies. Each of the eight had its own stockholders and boards of directors, and they became competitors. The seven regional companies created a common organization to carry out certain responsibilities. Projects which had been in the old Bell Laboratories were assigned either to the new Bell Laboratories or the new organization, and the people working on the projects went with the projects. My project went to the new organization. The work stayed the same, but budgeting changed. The Business Information Systems budget was set by a 23-person committee, with one person from each operating telephone company. In the new organization, there were many seven-person committees, one committee member from each Regional company, which established the budget. I made many speeches to the 23-person committee, and several of the seven-person committees. I never had an opportunity to speak to a board of directors, but I often thought of the advice I got from the school superintendent when I prepared those speeches.

The organization I became part of went through several names. When it was created, it was called the Central Services Organization. Later it became Bell Communications Research, which was later shortened to

Bellcore. After my retirement, it was renamed Telcordia, and sold by the seven regional companies to a company called Scientific Applications International. Scientific Applications International later sold it again.

Shortly before I retired, I had an opportunity to spend two weeks visiting Bellsouth, in Atlanta and surrounding areas. The purpose of the visit was to increase my understanding of telephone company operations, so I could do a better job of meeting telephone company needs in my work. At the end of the two weeks, I realized almost every job we heard described either involved entering information into computers or using information from computers to carry out tasks. So we had really accomplished our goal of computerizing the telephone business. It had taken us 26 years.

During the course of my career, I wrote, either by myself or with co-authors, eleven technical papers or journal articles. I also wrote part of the section on operations systems for a reference book[4].

During my entire career, we never had a layoff. We were always recruiting at least enough to replace losses, and almost always to grow slightly. That is no longer true, and people I used to work with have had to deal with layoffs.

I retired in 1993. It was a little sooner than I wanted to retire, but several things occurred that made retiring at that time desirable. The organization I had been in when I worked on the Service Control Point put on a nice retirement party for me.

---

[4]   Engineering and Operations in the Bell System, by Members of the Technical Staff and the Technical Publication Department, published in 1984

After retirement, I had two consulting assignments, each lasting about three months. One was with Ameritech, the Regional Bell Operating Company in the Midwest. The other was with Teligent, a start-up telephone company competing with the Bell companies. The assignment with Teligent was from December, 1999, to February, 2000. I haven't had any opportunities since, so my technical career is over.

PERSONAL LIFE—NEWARK, NEW PROVIDENCE, AND MIDDLETOWN

Of course, I had a personal life in parallel with my work life. I choose to describe them separately, although they happened at the same time.

When I accepted employment with Bell Telephone Laboratories in Murray Hill, New Jersey, the company's relocation staff lined up a furnished apartment for us in the Ivy Hill Apartments in Newark, New Jersey (near South Orange). We drove our 1950 Oldsmobile across the country, and the company shipped our meager belongings for us. Ivy Hill was a complex of six 15-floor buildings. We were on the fourth floor of one of these. Living in close proximity to so many people was a new experience for us, but we had no trouble adjusting to the environment.

The drive from Ivy Hill to Murray Hill was about fifteen miles, and the path went through ten different towns. Having all these towns so close together was another big difference from the West. There were quite a few Bell Laboratories people in the Ivy Hill Apartments, and we got acquainted with many of them. In particular, Dave Carlson, his wife

Theresa, Al Roberts, his wife Ruth, and Ralph Roberts, and his wife, Janet, became life-long friends. Ralph and Janet died some years ago, and Al died in 2007, but we remain close with the survivors to this day. Dave and Theresa were anxious to get into a house, and they found one in Holmdel, New Jersey. Al and Ralph and their families moved to South Plainfield, but the distances didn't interfere with our friendship.

Our first child, Brian Neil Bowyer, was born September 26, 1957. Since we expected to be living closer to Murray Hill, we found an obstetrician in Summit, New Jersey, and Brian was born in Summit.

Brian at One Year

When we arrived in New Jersey, I believe our total net worth consisted of $500 cash. By the time Brian was born, we had scraped together enough money to buy him a crib. By the next spring, we had enough money to buy some furniture, so we looked for an unfurnished apartment. We found what we needed at 23 Gales Drive, New Providence, New Jersey. It was nice and close to work (I often walked to work), and it was on the first floor of a two-story building, referred to as a garden apartment. We joined the New Providence United Methodist Church.

Our second child, Ellen Sue Bowyer, was born January 26, 1960. We were still using the same obstetrician as for Brian, and Ellen was also born in Summit. Margie's sister, Janet, came from Detroit, where she lived at the time, to help us at the time of the birth.

Ellen as a Young Dancer

In 1960, my mother was diagnosed with cancer. In the fall of 1960, at one point my father told me her prognosis was poor, so I told him we would plan to come home at Christmas time. He reported that to the doctor, who told him, "They'd better come at Thanksgiving, instead." We did, and had a wonderful last visit with her. She was able to get acquainted with Brian and Ellen. She died December 12, 1960.

In 1962, the organization I was part of was moved from Murray Hill to Holmdel, New Jersey, about forty miles away. This was far enough that the company was willing to pay our moving expenses, and by this point we wanted to live in a house, so the move was very convenient for us. We found a house we liked at 4 Ned Court in Middletown. It was about a twenty-minute drive from work, and in a very nice neighborhood. The house had a main floor above grade level, containing four bedrooms, kitchen, and living room-dining room combination. Slightly below grade level was a finished recreation room, an unfinished storage room, and a two-car garage.

Our House in Middletown

We now lived close to the Carlsons, and the two Roberts families also moved to Middletown, so our friendship strengthened. We met Bob and Marion Andrews at a "parent's night at school" event, where Brian and their son, David, were in the same class, and the Andrews became life-long friends. For years, we had a Thanksgiving tradition of dinner with the Carlsons and the Andrews. The Carlsons were from Illinois, and the Andrews were from Washington State, so we were all far from our families.

Our second son, Andrew Clarke Bowyer, was born January 26, 1963, at Riverview Hospital in Red Bank, New Jersey, the nearest town to where we lived. Janet Roberts looked after our older two children while Margie and I were busy with the birth.

Andy at 2

We joined the Red Bank United Methodist Church. In about 1964, at the request of the bishop, a new church was formed, and we became charter members of the Middletown United Methodist Church. Initially, we met in a school. After we left Middletown, the church constructed a beautiful building, which we have been back to visit a few times.

While we were in Middletown, I became a member of the Jaycees. One of the objectives of Jaycees is to develop leadership, but I chose to play the role of being the person other members could practice leading.

Margie has always been busy in lots of activities, showing a lot more talent for that than I have. Rather than reporting those activities in this section, I will report them in a section following.

We established a tradition of driving home to Colorado every two years. Margie would fix a casserole, load the kids and the luggage in the station wagon, and pick me up at work on a Friday afternoon. The back seats would be folded flat, so the kids and the person not driving could lie down. We would head west, only stopping for fuel and Saturday meals, arriving in Colorado Springs before sunup on Sunday morning. We would divide our time between Colorado Springs and Longmont, and then leave on a Saturday morning to head back to New Jersey. Both of us would prefer to drive rather than dealing with the kids, and we took turns doing the two duties. We had a little train case that we would put next to the driver, and sometimes one of the kids would sit there to chat with the driver while everyone else was asleep. In those days, cars didn't have seat belts, and car-seats for babies didn't exist, so traveling was a little simpler than it is today. It was a wonderful change the first time we made the trip without having to change diapers. Diapers were cloth in those days, so they had to be stored till we got to our destination, to be washed and reused.

The years we didn't go to Colorado, we took a "real" vacation. We went various places. One year we went to Maine, and rented a place beside a lake. Another time we went to Lake of the Ozarks.

A tradition we started in about 1963 was staying at the New Jersey shore for a week every year. Al Roberts was part of an extended family that owns a house in Ocean City. He would arrange to rent it the last week of June, and the two Roberts families, the Carlsons, and we, would stay there for the week. The house has seven bedrooms, and a dining room that can seat about twenty people, so there was space to accommodate our growing families. During many of the years we were there, Ralph and Janet had four kids, and the other three families had three each.

Because we enjoyed Ocean City so much, in 1980 the Carlsons and we bought a house in Ocean City, primarily as an investment. For years, the investment would have been a net loss if we had sold. We sold it in 2007, at a modest profit.

The house we owned in Ocean City

PERSONAL LIFE—RANDOLPH

When I joined Data Trends in 1966, my office was in Parsippany, about fifty miles north of Middletown, so we moved. We found a house at 37 Radke Road, Randolph, New Jersey. The house was virtually identical to our house in Middletown, but maybe three feet larger. It was in the community around Shongum Lake, which was part of the attraction of moving there. Shongum Lake had swimming and boating (and ice skating most years), and there was a community organized around a club house.

Our House in Randolph

Brian was in third grade and Ellen was in kindergarten when we moved. They adjusted quickly to the new schools and the new neighborhood.

We joined the Millbrook United Methodist Church when we arrived. It was a small country church, much like the church in Hugo, but much different from the Colorado Springs church Margie was used to. At Millbrook, it was almost impossible to be a pew-sitter—everyone needed to help in the administration of the church. Between us, we held most all the offices a local United Methodist Church has over the course of the years—administrative board, finance, missions, and so on.

I served two terms on the Shongum Lake Property Owners Association Board of Directors, including one term as treasurer and one term as president. That was about the extent of my community activities.

In 1971, we took a very interesting trip. We visited France, Holland, Belgium, and England. Margie's parents were in Cornwall, England, at the time, so Tom was able to show us where he had lived and attended church prior to moving to North America. I came home after two weeks, because I only had that much vacation, and the rest of the family stayed on for a while.

Brian graduated from Randolph High School in 1975, and enrolled in the University of Colorado, majoring in chemical engineering. We were pleased that he chose to go to the school we had attended. By coincidence, he was assigned to the dormitory we had lived in during our senior year. The following summer, he had a job as a life guard at the Randolph municipal swimming facility, which was on a lake. On July 18, he went swimming on his break, and dived down near the anchored floats that marked the boundary of the swimming area. He became tangled in the ropes, and drowned. I have never recovered from this loss.

Margie, Andy, Ellen, Brian, and Ray in 1976

During the summer of 1976, Ellen accomplished a dream she had for a long time, by traveling to England with a friend, Pam Knight. It was a wonderful experience for her. It was unfortunate that she was there at the time of Brian's death. She chose to continue with her plans, which I think was the right thing to do.

Late in 1976, some good friends of ours, Tom and Ginny Smith, were transferred from Randolph to Florida. They were foster parents at the time for Timothy and Doreen Cooper, a brother and sister. Since the kids were wards of the state of New Jersey, they couldn't be taken to Florida. After some soul-searching, we offered to become foster parents of Tim and Doreen, and our offer was accepted. In 1978, they became eligible for adoption. We adopted Tim, and the Smiths adopted Doreen. Tim has been a wonderful son for us, and we consider Doreen a daughter. We stay very close to Doreen and her family.

Tim at the time he came to us

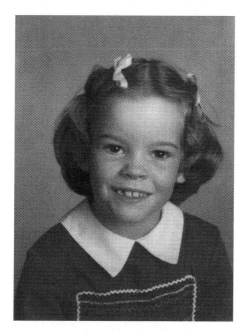

Doreen when she lived with us

Brian started Cub Scouts as soon as he was eligible, and stayed in the Scouting program the whole time he lived in Randolph, reaching the rank of Eagle Scout. Ellen was in Girl Scouts the whole time she was eligible, earning First Class, which was the top award in Girl Scouts at the time. Andy went through Indian Guides, Cub Scouts, and started in Boy Scouts, but he lost interest before he reached Eagle Scout. Tim was a Cub Scout and Boy Scout most of the time he was eligible. I was Cubmaster for a while, and served on both the Cub Scout and the Boy Scout committees at different times.

Doreen, Andy, Margie, Ellen, Ray, Tim

Scott and Ellen

Ellen graduated from Randolph High School in 1978, and chose to attend Duke University in Durham, North Carolina. It was a wonderful choice for her. She started with a major in electrical engineering, and changed to computer science prior to graduation. She graduated in 1982, and that same year married Scott Harward. They have a wonderful family. They moved to Marietta, near Atlanta, Georgia, in 1986, and have lived there ever since. Scott is an independent consultant in sales and marketing, and Ellen is the administrative assistant to a middle school principal.

Andy and Dolores

Andy graduated from Randolph High School in 1981, and chose to attend Pennsylvania State University, majoring in business marketing. The year 1986 was a special year for us with all three of our kids—Ellen had our first grandchild, Andy graduated from Penn State, and Tim graduated from Randolph High School. The year 1996 was a special year for Andy—he bought his first house, married Dolores Hannon, and had his first child. They also have a wonderful family. They have lived in Wayne, New Jersey, since their marriage. Andy works as a service writer for a car dealer, and Dolores works as a project manager at Comcast, the cable company, which also provides telephone service.

Tim

Tim obtained an associate degree from DeVry Institute (now DeVry University) in 1988. He worked for a few years, and then decided to return to DeVry to work for a bachelor's degree. At the time, DeVry didn't offer the bachelor's degree in New Jersey, so he enrolled in the Georgia branch of DeVry, from which he received his degree in 1996. He has lived in Georgia ever since. He has worked for several companies as a manufacturer's representative or field technician. He bought his first house in 2003.

In 1987, Margie and I made a trip to New Zealand, accompanied by my brother, Dean, and his wife, Sharon. We hiked the Milford Track, which takes about five days. We also made contact with several friends and relatives who live in New Zealand. One family deserves special discussion. In 1863, two great-uncles of Tom Clarke had emigrated to Timaru, New Zealand, from Cornwall. Contact had been lost with the family until 1963, when Tom and Isabel tracked down some of their descendants;

in particular, a great-grandson of one of the great-uncles, named Arthur Clarke. Arthur and his wife, Margaret, were gracious hosts on this visit, and we remain in close contact to this day.

We have been active square dancers for many years. Margie had danced both in high school and college, so dancing is deeply ingrained in her. We took classes twice with the Ironia Reelers Square Dance Club in Randolph, and were active members for fifteen years or so before moving.

I developed an interest in family history and genealogy. I found that it was impossible for me to accurately record the information with a typewriter. After I bought my first personal computer in 1975, it became feasible to record the information. Eventually, I published two books, one on my family and one on Margie's family[5]. They are both in the Library of Congress and many libraries with genealogy sections, and I have sold about fifty copies to interested people.

I have become the record-keeper for three family reunion groups—the Bowyer and Lyness families (related through my grandfather, Pem Bowyer, and his wife, Josie Lyness), the Skavdahl and Wickersham families (related through my grandfather, Oscar Skavdahl, and his wife, Grace Wickersham), and the Hansford and Hambly families (related through Margie's grandfather, Alfred Hansford, and his wife, Elizabeth Jane Hambly). I keep a mailing list of all people we know eligible for each group, and send out the letters inviting people to attend family reunions. I also print out the family tree for each reunion in a chart that is typically about twenty feet long, to mount on the wall for the attendees to look at.

---

[5] Clarke-Hansford Genealogy, published December 1, 1996, and Bowyer-Skavdahl Genealogy, published April 15, 1999.

I also edit a Bowyer-Lyness newsletter, which is published several times a year.

I developed an interest in sailing, first on Shongum Lake, and later on the ocean. Margie, my brother Dean, his wife Sharon, Andy, and I, took a sailing course in the British Virgin Islands in 1978, and for many years I sailed for a week each year. Here are some of my more significant voyages:

- In 1988, Margie and I sailed with our friends, Ron and Ellie Robb, off the coast of Maine.
- In 1989, Margie and I sailed with our friends, Bob and Maria Rathbun, and the owner of the boat we were on, from Destin, Florida, to Isla Mujares, Mexico.
- In 1990, we sailed with Margie's niece, Jane Richey, and her husband, Dave, from Santa Barbara, California, to the Channel Islands, around the islands, and back to Santa Barbara.
- In 1991, Dean, Andy, two friends, and I sailed from Barnegat Bay (in New Jersey) to Montauk Point (at the eastern tip of Long Island, New York) and back.
- In 1994, I sailed with Bob and Maria Rathbun from Melbourne, Florida, to Fajardo, at the eastern tip of Puerto Rico.
- That same year, we sailed with Andy and our friend, David Andrews, in and around the San Juan Islands of Washington State.
- In 1997, Margie and I sailed with three friends from Miami, Florida, to the Bahamas and back.
- In 1998, Margie and I sailed from the United States Virgin Islands to Norfolk, Virginia with our friends, Dick and Ellen Robrock.

A typical sailboat we chartered

MARGIE'S ACTIVITIES

Margie's activities are significant enough they deserve a section of their own. In college, she was in Spur, a sophomore women's organization, in Chi Omega sorority, in Psi Chi, the psychology honorary, and in many such things as homecoming and spring festival planning committees.

After college, she has been active every place we have lived in Chi Omega alumna activities. The Chi Omega alumna of Georgia act as guides at the governor's mansion, among other things.

She was active in the American Association of University Women in Middletown and in Randolph. The other places we have lived have not had active groups.

When Ellen was ready to start Girl Scouts, she became a Girl Scout leader. After several years of being a troop leader, she was recruited to be a consultant for several troops. Eventually, she was invited to join the board of directors of the Morris Area Girl Scout Council, which was the council that included Randolph. She served one term as president of that Council. After leaving the board, she became a Council Communicator, responsible for coordinating the activities of several councils. She was then invited to join the Board of Directors of the Girl Scouts of the USA. After leaving that board, she was asked to join the World Foundation for Girl Guides and Girl Scouts, where she remains today. She also joined the Olave Baden-Powell Society, an international Girl Guide/Girl Scout organization.

After we were foster parents of Tim and Doreen, Margie learned about and became part of an organization called the Child Placement Review Board. This board meets regularly to review the status of all children who are wards of the state for any reason. They make recommendations to the juvenile judges of what action should be taken, if any, with regard to these children. When she moved to Georgia, she became part of the corresponding board in our county.

When Tim no longer needed her care at home, she went to work. She worked as Director of Volunteers at several nearby hospitals at different times, and she worked for an organization dedicated to helping people find good matches for their talents with other organizations.

RETIREMENT

After I retired in 1993, my place of employment no longer determined where we should live. Since Ellen and Tim lived in Georgia at the time, we decided to move to Georgia. After exploring several areas in Georgia, we chose a community called Big Canoe. It is a gated community, about sixty miles north of downtown Atlanta and 38 miles north of where Scott and Ellen live. It has proved to be a wonderful place to live.

Our House in Big Canoe

Margie followed her normal pattern and immediately got involved in many organizations—Ridge Runners (the women's club of Big Canoe), Chapel Guild (a women's organization allied with the Big Canoe Chapel), the Chi Omega alumna group, and others. She became a volunteer at Northside Hospital (on the north side of Atlanta, about fifty miles away) and with Georgia Mountains Hospice. Her leadership skills were recognized by becoming president of Ridge Runners, a board member of the Big Canoe Home Owners Association (including being vice president), and a board member of Georgia Mountains Hospice (including being vice president). She was chosen as Big Canoe Woman of the Year in 2002. Together, we have helped the chapel as ushers, as communion stewards, and as helpers with the coffee hour held between services. We were both on the committee to welcome and introduce new members to the chapel for several years.

I have participated in a few activities. Shortly after moving to Big Canoe, I was asked to join the board of directors of the Friends of the Pickens County Library, and I have been on this board ever since. In 2001, I became the membership record keeper for the Friends, and in 2010 I was elected chairperson. I was selected to be chairperson of the property committee of the Big Canoe Chapel, and it happened we had a terrible storm (November 11, 2002), which damaged the chapel and its grounds seriously, while I held this office. I coordinated the efforts to repair and restore the chapel and its grounds. I have been a volunteer operator of the sound system at the Big Canoe Chapel about once a month for several years. I became a reporter for the Big Canoe newsletter, Smoke Signals, and normally write one or more articles for each issue. I was elected to the board of directors of the Big Canoe Home Owners Association, and served as secretary. I joined a group called the Big Canoe Emergency Response Team, and helped in the response to several fires and two missing persons cases. I joined a group called Dawson County Community Response Team, and participated in several emergencies with that group.

I decided I wanted to find an activity that would provide some income, that would give me the opportunity to use my brain, but that wouldn't be a full-time activity. The activity that fit those requirements was to become a tax preparer for H&R Block. I had no qualifications for such a position, but the owner of the Jasper franchise (in the nearest town to Big Canoe) was willing to give me a job. I have worked there every tax season since we moved to Big Canoe, with two exceptions. One year, the consulting job at Teligent got in the way, and one year the trip to New Jersey to help at the time of Clare's birth got in the way. In the Jasper office, the peak of the season is January 25 to February 20, because most of our clients get a refund, and they want their refund as soon as possible. I have enjoyed the work, and enjoyed the opportunity to learn about the tax laws. I have picked up a few clients on the side, whom I do returns for, some for pay and some I do as a gift.

We have played bridge all our married lives. Margie had learned the game at home, and I learned during our senior year in college. During our early married years, it provided an inexpensive entertainment and a way to socialize with friends. When we first moved to Big Canoe, we played with a couples group that plays every Monday evening. We dropped out of that group because of the press of other activities, but as I write this, Margie plays with two women's groups and we play together in a duplicate bridge group that meets once a month.

We have continued square dancing, but not nearly as actively as in Randolph. In Big Canoe, the good dances are all an hour's drive away.

Because of the distance, we usually stop for a meal on the way. So we use five hours of our time to dance two hours, and that is less fun than when we used to be able to get to Reelers dances in fifteen minutes. Currently, we dance with the Bent Tree Twirlers (about ten miles away), although their level of skill isn't what we're used to.

We have traveled quite a bit since retiring. We went on several Caribbean cruises, all with square dance groups. We drive west about every two years, to attend family reunions in Colorado, Nebraska, or Canada, or some combination. We drive back to New Jersey, usually to visit Andy and his family, about twice a year. We made the following major trips:

- In 1996, we traveled to Norway, where we made contact with many of my Norwegian relatives, and then took a cruise to all the Scandinavian capitols.
- In 1998, we participated in a trip to Thailand and Indonesia with some chapel friends.
- In 1999, we took a tour of Alaska. This provided us the opportunity to visit with one of my best friends from high school, Don Gotschall, and his wife, Marion.
- In 2000, we traveled to the Passion Play in Oberammergau with a group of people, mostly from the Big Canoe chapel. On that trip, we also spent some time in Cornwall, England, to visit family.
- In 2001, we traveled through the eastern and south-eastern portions of Australia.
- In 2004, we made a return trip to New Zealand.

We are members of an organization called Friendship Force. The objective of Friendship Force is to create friendships between people of different countries. A club in one country visits a club in a different country, staying in their homes and being shown the sights. We have hosted some people from other countries, and have traveled with Friendship Force to Germany, Norway, Ireland, Australia, Japan, Canada, and South Africa. We have both held several offices, including president.

I have become quite active in developing World Wide Web sites. The first one, which I got involved with in 1998, was a web site dedicated to family, created by my cousin, Neil Lenker, who is related to me through my mother. I started working with him to improve and add to his site. The following year, I created a very similar site for the people related to Margie or me, but not to Neil. At Margie's request, I created a site for the World Foundation for Girl Guides and Girl Scouts in 1998, and continue to maintain it today. In 2000, I was asked to create web sites for the Big Canoe Home Owners Association and the Big Canoe Chapel. I did, and later the two organizations assigned the maintenance work to someone else. In 2003, I took over the web site for the Friendship Force of Big Canoe-North Georgia, and still maintain it. I created a web site for the Friends of the Pickens County Library. As I write this, I have partial responsibility for the web site of the Good Samaritan Health and Wellness Center.

We had a wonderful fiftieth-anniversary celebration in 2006. Here is what our family looked like at that time:

Back row: Dolores Bowyer, Andy Bowyer, Tim Bowyer, Ellen Harward, Scott
Harward, Michael Harward, Kevin Harward
Front row: Luke Bowyer, Matthew Bowyer, Clare Bowyer, Margie,
Ray, Philip Harward

Since that time, the family has grown by two new granddaughters-in-law:

Lara and Kevin

Laura Beth and Michael

CONCLUSION

I hope you have found my description of my life interesting. I have had the privilege of seeing many changes take place, and of playing a small role in some of them through my employment. I would enjoy hearing from anyone who comes across this book.

raybowyer@earthlink.net